THE STORY OF HALF-CHICKEN

A Folktale from
Spain and Latin America

THE STORY OF HALF-CHICKEN

A Folktale from
Spain and Latin America

Retold and Illustrated by Ivar Da Coll

HOUGHTON MIFFLIN   BOSTON • MORRIS PLAINS, NJ

California • Colorado • Georgia • Illinois • New Jersey • Texas

The Story of Half-Chicken, retold and illustrated by Ivar Da Coll.

Copyright © 2001 by Houghton Mifflin Company. All rights reserved.

No part of this work may be reproduced or transmitted in any form or by any means, electronic or mechanical, including photocopying and recording, or by any information storage or retrieval system without the prior written permission of the copyright owner unless such copying is expressly permitted by federal copyright law. With the exception of nonprofit transcription in Braille, Houghton Mifflin is not authorized to grant permission for further uses of this work. Permission must be obtained from the individual copyright owner as identified herein. Address requests for permission to make copies of Houghton Mifflin material to School Permissions, Houghton Mifflin Company, 222 Berkeley Street, Boston, MA 02116

PRINTED IN THE U.S.A.

ISBN: 0-618-03446-3

11 12 13 14 15 16 17—B—07 06 05

Once upon a time long ago, a kind little chicken
lived a simple life on the farm. Because he flew
with only one wing and hopped on just one leg,
his friends called him Half-Chicken.

One day, the farmer's wife said, "Half-Chicken is so special. If only we had the time to take him to meet the king."

Half-Chicken overheard this and was very proud.
And so one sunny day, hippity! hop! hippity! hop!
he set off for the palace all by himself.

Soon he came upon a campfire that was
burned nearly down to embers.

"Help! Help!" cried Fire. "My flame is dying
out. Fan me quickly so that the meal will be
cooked when the campers return."

"I'll help," said Half-Chicken. And with his
one wing, he flapped and flapped, fanning the
flame until it burned brightly once more.

"Thank you, Half-Chicken," said Fire. "I won't forget your kindness."

"You're welcome," said Half-Chicken. And he hippity-hopped away.

Before long he came to a river tangled with
fallen branches.

"Help! Help!" cried Water. "A storm left these branches in a heap, and they won't let me pass."

"I'll help," said Half-Chicken. And with his one wing, he pushed and pulled, and soon a path opened for the water to flow through again.

"Thank you, Half-Chicken," said Water. "I won't forget your kindness."

"You're welcome," said Half-Chicken. And he hippity-hopped away.

Then he came to a great clearing in the
woods where he saw a giant cloud of dust
swirling in a circle.

"Help! Help!" cried Wind. "I was playing in this clearing, but now I can't find my way out."

"I'll help," said Half-Chicken. And he hopped
on his one leg through the thicket and found a
path wide enough for the wind to make its way.

"Thank you, Half-Chicken," said Wind. "I won't forget your kindness."

"You're welcome," said Half-Chicken. And he hippity-hopped away.

At last, he came to the palace gates. It was market day, and the king's cook was setting off to shop for the royal meals. When he spied Half-Chicken, he was amazed! "Just what I need," he thought, "half a chicken to make a tasty soup for the king!"

17

Cook scooped up Half-Chicken, tucked him under
his arm, and carried him straight to the kitchen.

There, Half-Chicken watched nervously as Cook
lit a fire in the big, iron stove. Cook chopped up
carrots and onions and threw them into a pot
of water. Soon he popped Half-Chicken in as
well, closed the lid, and left.

"Help! Help!" cried Half-Chicken. "I don't like it here!
This is not why I came to see the king!"

Fire, Water, and Wind heard his cries. They came quickly.
"Half-Chicken," they said, "now it's our turn to help you!"

Fire hid deep and low so that Water wouldn't boil. Water splish-splashed, knocking the lid off the pot, and sloshing Half-Chicken out onto the floor.

Then Wind blew hard enough to carry Half-Chicken out of the palace, over the treetops, and onto the highest roof in the kingdom. Half-Chicken looked around and liked where he was so much that he stayed there

forever, turning each day to greet the wind. And all the people watched him to see which direction the wind was blowing from.

In fact, Half-Chicken became so famous that people wanted their own half-chickens to perch over barns and houses.

Today, weather vanes still point in the wind's direction. Next time you see one, think of the kindly Half-Chicken in this story.